ACCOUNTING PRINCIPLES

THIRD CANADIAN EDITION

ACCOUNTING PRINCIPLES

WORKING PAPERS

Part 2

Chapters 8-10

▶ **JERRY J. WEYGANDT** *Ph. D., C.P.A.*
Arthur Andersen Alumni Professor of Accounting
University of Wisconsin—Madison
Madison, Wisconsin

▶ **DONALD E. KIESO** *Ph. D., C.P.A.*
KPMG Peat Marwick Emeritus Professor of Accountancy
Northern Illinois University
DeKalb, Illinois

▶ **PAUL D. KIMMEL** *Ph. D., C.P.A.*
University of Wisconsin—Milwaukee
Milwaukee, Wisconsin

▶ **BARBARA TRENHOLM** *M.B.A., F.C.A.*
University of New Brunswick
Fredericton, New Brunswick

John Wiley & Sons Canada, Ltd.

National Library of Canada Cataloguing in Publication

Trenholm, Barbara A.
    Working papers to accompany Accounting principles, third Canadian edition / Barbara Trenholm.

ISBN 0-470-83458-7 (pt. 1).—ISBN 0-470-83459-5 (pt. 2)

    1. Accounting—Problems, exercises, etc. I. Title.

HF5635.A3778 2003 Suppl. 3   657'.044   C2003-907305-X

Production Credits
Publisher: John Horne
Publishing Services Director: Karen Bryan
Editorial Manager: Karen Staudinger
Senior Marketing Manager: Janine Daoust
Printing & Binding: Tri-Graphic Printing Limited

Printed and bound in Canada
10 9 8 7 6 5 4 3 2 1

John Wiley & Sons Canada, Ltd.
22 Worcester Road
Etobicoke, Ontario M9W 1L1

Visit our website at: www.wiley.com/canada

BE8-1

BE8-2 to 8-4

General Journal

Date	Account Titles and Explanation	Ref.	Debit	Credit

BE8-5

Number of Days Outstanding	Accounts Receivable	% Estimated Uncollectible	Estimated Bad Debts
0-30 days	$315,000	1%	
31-60 days	91,000	4%	
61-90 days	59,000	10%	
Over 90 days	35,000	20%	
Total	$500,000		

(Adjusting journal entry)

General Journal

Date	Account Titles and Explanation	Ref.	Debit	Credit

BE8-6 (a)

General Journal

Date	Account Titles and Explanation	Ref.	Debit	Credit

(b)

	(1) Before Write-Off	(2) After Write-Off

BE8-7 to 8-8

General Journal

Date	Account Titles and Explanation	Ref.	Debit	Credit

BE8-9

BE8-10

BE8-11

General Journal

Date	Account Titles and Explanation	Ref.	Debit	Credit

BE8-12

General Journal

Date	Account Titles and Explanation	Ref.	Debit	Credit

BE8-13 (a)

General Journal

Date	Account Titles and Explanation	Ref.	Debit	Credit

BE8-13 (b)

BE8-13 (c)

BE8-14

(a)

General Journal

Date	Account Titles and Explanation	Ref.	Debit	Credit

(b)   Subsidiary Ledger

Madison Canuel

Date	Explanation	Ref.	Debit	Credit	Balance

Elaine Davidson

Date	Explanation	Ref.	Debit	Credit	Balance

Andrew Noren

Date	Explanation	Ref.	Debit	Credit	Balance

Eric Smistad

Date	Explanation	Ref.	Debit	Credit	Balance

General Ledger

Accounts Receivable

Date	Explanation	Ref.	Debit	Credit	Balance

E8-1 (c)

E8-2

General Journal

Date	Account Titles and Explanation	Ref.	Debit	Credit

E8-3 (a)

Age of Accounts	Amount	% Estimated Uncollectible	Estimated Uncollectible
0-30 days outstanding		2%	
31-60 days outstanding		10%	
61-90 days outstanding		30%	
Over 90 days outstanding		50%	
Total			

(b)

General Journal

Date	Account Titles and Explanation	Ref.	Debit	Credit

E8-4 to 8-5

General Journal

Date	Account Titles and Explanation	Ref.	Debit	Credit

E8-6

E8-7 to 8-9

General Journal

Date	Account Titles and Explanation	Ref.	Debit	Credit

E8-10 (a)

General Journal

Date	Account Titles and Explanation	Ref.	Debit	Credit

E8-10 (b)

E8-11

(a)

(b)

(c)

(d)

E8-12

E8-13

(a) and (c)

General Journal

Date	Account Titles and Explanation	Ref.	Debit	Credit

(b)   Accounts Receivable

Date	Explanation	Ref.	Debit	Credit	Balance
Dec. 31	Balance				960,000

Allowance for Doubtful Accounts

Date	Explanation	Ref.	Debit	Credit	Balance
Dec. 31	Balance				70,000

(d)	

Section

Date

(a), (b) and (c)

General Journal

Date	Account Titles and Explanation	Ref.	Debit	Credit

(a) and (b)

Bad Debts Expense

Date	Explanation	Ref.	Debit	Credit	Balance

Allowance for Doubtful Accounts

Date	Explanation	Ref.	Debit	Credit	Balance
2004					
Dec. 31	Balance				14,000

(a)

Number of Days Outstanding	Amount	% Estimated Uncollectible	Estimated Uncollectible
0-30 days outstanding	$120,000	1%	
31-60 days outstanding	60,000	5%	
61-90 days outstanding	50,000	10%	
Over 90 days outstanding	30,000	20%	
Total	$260,000		

(b) to (d)

General Journal

Date	Account Titles and Explanation	Ref.	Debit	Credit

(e)

Name _____   Problem 8-5A

Section _____

Date _____

(a) to (c)

General Journal

Date	Account Titles and Explanation	Ref.	Debit	Credit

(d)

Accounts Receivable

Date	Explanation	Ref.	Debit	Credit	Balance
	Balance				200,000

Allowance for Doubtful Accounts

Date	Explanation	Ref.	Debit	Credit	Balance
	Balance				14,000

(e) to (f)

Section

Date

(g)   Accounts Receivable

Date	Explanation	Ref.	Debit	Credit	Balance
	Balance				200,000

Allowance for Doubtful Accounts

Date	Explanation	Ref.	Debit	Credit	Balance
	Balance				14,000

General Journal

Date	Account Titles and Explanation	Ref.	Debit	Credit

Accounts Receivable		Allowance for Doubtful Accounts	
Yr. 1 Bal.	8,450,000	725,000	Yr. 1 Bal.

General Journal

Date	Account Titles and Explanation	Ref.	Debit	Credit

(a) September

General Journal

Date	Account Titles and Explanation	Ref.	Debit	Credit

(a) October

General Journal

Date	Account Titles and Explanation	Ref.	Debit	Credit

(a) (Continued)

Accounts Receivable

Date	Explanation	Ref.	Debit	Credit	Balance
Aug. 31	Balance				742,500

Allowance for Doubtful Accounts

Date	Explanation	Ref.	Debit	Credit	Balance
Aug. 31	Balance				27,570

(b) to (c)	

General Journal				
Date	Account Titles and Explanation	Ref.	Debit	Credit

P8-8A

General Journal

Date	Account Titles and Explanation	Ref.	Debit	Credit

P8-9A

(a) General Journal

Date	Account Titles and Explanation	Ref.	Debit	Credit

(a) (Continued)

General Journal

Date	Account Titles and Explanation	Ref.	Debit	Credit

(b)

Notes Receivable

Date	Explanation	Ref.	Debit	Credit	Balance
Oct. 1	Balance				25,200

Accounts Receivable

Date	Explanation	Ref.	Debit	Credit	Balance

Interest Receivable

Date	Explanation	Ref.	Debit	Credit	Balance
Oct. 1	Balance				155

P8-9A (c)

(d)

General Journal

Date	Account Titles and Explanation	Ref.	Debit	Credit

P8-10A

	Rogers	Shaw
Receivables turnover:		
Average collection period:		

(a) to (b)

General Journal

Date	Account Titles and Explanation	Ref.	Debit	Credit

Section

Date

(c)

Accounts Receivable

Date	Explanation	Ref.	Debit	Credit	Balance
Dec. 31	Balance				995,000

Allowance for Doubtful Accounts

Date	Explanation	Ref.	Debit	Credit	Balance
Dec. 31	Balance				62,500

(d)

(a)

		Number of Days Outstanding			
	Total	0-30	31-60	61-90	91-120
Total	$285,000	$162,000	$32,000	$26,000	$65,000
Estimated percentage uncollectible		4%	8%	12%	25%
Estimated bad debts					

(b) to (d)

General Journal

Date	Account Titles and Explanation	Ref.	Debit	Credit

Section

Date

(a)

	Total	Number of Days Outstanding			
		0-30	31-60	61-90	91-120
Total	$385,000	$220,000	$100,000	$40,000	$25,000
Estimated percentage uncollectible		1%	4%	8%	25%
Estimated bad debts					

(b) to (d)

General Journal

Date	Account Titles and Explanation	Ref.	Debit	Credit

(e) to (f)

(a), (b), (c) and (g)

General Journal

Date	Account Titles and Explanation	Ref.	Debit	Credit

(b), (d), (e), (f) and (g)

	Accounts Receivable		Allowance for Doubtful Accounts	
Yr. 1 Bal.	3,250,000		227,500	Yr. 1 Bal.

General Journal

Date	Account Titles and Explanation	Ref.	Debit	Credit

(a) April

General Journal

Date	Account Titles and Explanation	Ref.	Debit	Credit

(a) May

General Journal

Date	Account Titles and Explanation	Ref.	Debit	Credit

(a) (Continued)

Accounts Receivable

Date	Explanation	Ref.	Debit	Credit	Balance
March 31	Balance				892,500

Allowance for Doubtful Accounts

Date	Explanation	Ref.	Debit	Credit	Balance
March 31	Balance				47,750

(b) to (c)	

(a)

General Journal

Date	Account Titles and Explanation	Ref.	Debit	Credit

(a) (Continued)

General Journal

Date	Account Titles and Explanation	Ref.	Debit	Credit

(b)

(a)

(b)

General Journal

Date	Account Titles and Explanation	Ref.	Debit	Credit

(c)

Notes Receivable

Date	Explanation	Ref.	Debit	Credit	Balance
July 1	Balance				19,800

Accounts Receivable

Date	Explanation	Ref.	Debit	Credit	Balance

Interest Receivable

Date	Explanation	Ref.	Debit	Credit	Balance
July 1	Balance				87

(d)

(e)

Section

Date

	Nike	Reebok
Receivables turnover:		
Average collection period:		

(a)

(b)

General Journal

Date	Account Titles and Explanation	Ref.	Debit	Credit

BE9-1

BE9-2

BE9-3

General Journal

Date	Account Titles and Explanation	Ref.	Debit	Credit

BE9-4

BE9-5

BE9-10	
(a)	Repaired building roof, $500
(b)	Replaced building roof, $7,500
(c)	Purchased building, $80,000
(d)	Purchased supplies, $350
(e)	Purchased truck, $35,000
(f)	Purchased oil and gas for truck, $75
(g)	Replaced tires on truck, $500
(h)	Rebuilt engine on truck, $5,000
(i)	Added a new wing to building, $250,000
(j)	Painted interior of building, $1,500

BE9-11 to 9-12

General Journal

Date	Account Titles and Explanation	Ref.	Debit	Credit

BE9-13 to 9-14 (a)

General Journal

Date	Account Titles and Explanation	Ref.	Debit	Credit

BE9-14 (b)

BE9-15 (a) and (b)

General Journal

Date	Account Titles and Explanation	Ref.	Debit	Credit

BE9-15 (c)

BE9-16

(a)	Patent	(i)	Cut and processed timber
(b)	Land	(j)	Trademark
(c)	Building	(k)	Franchise
(d)	Cash	(l)	Investment in common shares
(e)	Licence right	(m)	Oil well
(f)	Machinery	(n)	Coal mine
(g)	Inventory	(o)	Natural gas deposit
(h)	Timber tract	(p)	Goodwill

BE9-17

BE9-18

E9-1

E9-2

E9-3 (a) and (c)	

E9-3 (b)

General Journal

Date	Account Titles and Explanation	Ref.	Debit	Credit

E9-4 (a) (1) Straight-line

	Calculation					End of Year	
Year	Amortizable Cost	X	Amortization Rate	=	Amortization Expense	Accumulated Amortization	Net Book Value
2004							
2005							
2006							
2007							

E9-4 (a) (Continued) (2) Double Declining-Balance

Year	Calculation					End of Year	
	Net Book Value Begin. of Year	X	Amortization Rate	=	Amortization Expense	Accumulated Amortization	Net Book Value
2004							
2005							
2006							
2007							

E9-4 (a) (3) Units-of-Activity

Year	Calculation					End of Year	
	Units of Activity	X	Amortization Cost/Unit	=	Amortization Expense	Accumulated Amortization	Net Book Value
2004							
2005							
2006							
2007							

E9-4 (b)

E9-5 (a) (1) Straight-line

Year	Calculation					End of Year	
	Amortizable Cost	X	Amortization Rate	=	Amortization Expense	Accumulated Amortization	Net Book Value
2004							
2005							
2006							
2007							
2008							
2009							

(a) (Continued) (2) Double Declining-Balance

Year	Calculation Net Book Value Begin. of Year	X	Amortization Rate	=	Amortization Expense	End of Year Accumulated Amortization	Net Book Value
2004							
2005							
2006							
2007							
2008							
2009							

(a) (3) Units-of-Activity

Year	Calculation Units of Activity	X	Amortization Cost/Unit	=	Amortization Expense	End of Year Accumulated Amortization	Net Book Value
2004							
2005							
2006							
2007							
2008							
2009							

(b) and (c)

(a) and (b)

(c)

General Journal

Date	Account Titles and Explanation	Ref.	Debit	Credit

	General Journal			
Date	Account Titles and Explanation	Ref.	Debit	Credit

E9-10 (a)

General Journal

Date	Account Titles and Explanation	Ref.	Debit	Credit

E9-10 (b)

E9-11

E9-12	General Journal			
Date	Account Titles and Explanation	Ref.	Debit	Credit

E9-13 (a)	Accounts	Financial Statement	Section
Accumulated amortization - buildings			
Accumulated amortization - finite-life intangible assets			
Accumulated amortization - machinery and equipment			
Accumulated amortization - other property, plant and equipment			
Accumulated amortization - telecommunications assets			
Amortization expense			
Buildings			
Cash and cash equivalents			
Cash paid for capital expenditures			
Common shares			
Finite-life intangible assets			
Goodwill			
Impairment charge			
Indefinite-life intangible assets			
Land			
Machinery and equipment			
Other long-term assets			
Other property, plant and equipment			
Plant under construction			
Telecommunications assets			

(b)

(a)

	2002	2001
Asset turnover		
Return on assets		

(b)

P9-1A

Item	Land	Land Improvements	Building	Other Accounts
1.				
2.				
3.				
4.				
5.				
6.				
7.				
8.				
9.				
10.				
11.				

P9-2A (a)

Year	Calculation
	MACHINE 1
2002	
2003	
2004	
2005	
	MACHINE 2
2003	
2004	
2005	
	MACHINE 3
2004	
2005	

(b)

Year	Calculation
	MACHINE 1
2002	
2003	
2004	
2005	
	MACHINE 2
2003	
2004	
2005	
	MACHINE 3
2004	
2005	

(c) and (d)

(a)

(b) 1. Straight-line

Year	Amortizable Cost	X	Amortization Rate	=	Amortization Expense	Accumulated Amortization	Net Book Value
2003							
2004							
2005							
2006							
2007							

(b) 2. Double Declining-Balance

Year	Net Book Value Begin. of Year	X	Amortization Rate	=	Amortization Expense	Accumulated Amortization	Net Book Value
2003							
2004							
2005							
2006							
2007							

(b) 3. Units-of-Activity

	Calculation				End of Year	
Year	Units of Activity	X	Amortization Cost/Unit	=	Amortization Expense	Accumulated Amortization	Net Book Value
2003							
2004							
2005							
2006							
2007							

(c) to (e)

(a) Straight-line

| Year | Calculation | | | | End of Year | |
	Amortizable Cost	X	Amortization Rate	= Amortization Expense	Accumulated Amortization	Net Book Value
2002						
2003						
2004						
2005						
2006						
2007						

(b)

No.	Account Debited	Explanation

(a)

General Journal

Date	Account Titles and Explanation	Ref.	Debit	Credit

(b) and (c)

(a) (1) Straight-line

Year	Amortizable Cost	X	Amortization Rate	=	Amortization Expense	Accumulated Amortization	Net Book Value
	Calculation					End of Year	
1							
2							
3							
4							
Total							

(2) Single Declining-Balance

Year	Net Book Value Begin. of Year	X	Amortization Rate	=	Amortization Expense	Accumulated Amortization	Net Book Value
	Calculation					End of Year	
1							
2							
3							
4							
Total							

(b)

General Journal				
Date	Account Titles and Explanation	Ref.	Debit	Credit

(a)

General Journal

Date	Account Titles and Explanation	Ref.	Debit	Credit

(b)

(c)

	General Journal			
Date	Account Titles and Explanation	Ref.	Debit	Credit

Name

Section

Date

(a) and (b)

General Journal

Date	Account Titles and Explanation	Ref.	Debit	Credit

(c)

(a)

General Journal

Date	Account Titles and Explanation	Ref.	Debit	Credit

P9-12A (b)

(c)

P9-13A (a)

	Audruski Company	Brar Company
Asset turnover		
Return on assets		

(b)

P9-1B

General Journal

Date	Account Titles and Explanation	Ref.	Debit	Credit

P9-2B (a)

Year	Calculation
	MACHINE 1
2001	
2002	
2003	
2004	
2005	
	MACHINE 2
2003	
2004	
2005	

(a) (Continued)

Year	Calculation
	MACHINE 3
2004	
2005	

(b)

Year	Calculation
	MACHINE 1
2001	
2002	
2003	
2004	
2005	
	MACHINE 2
2003	
2004	
2005	
	MACHINE 3
2004	
2005	

(c) and (d)

(a)

(b) 1. Straight-line

	Calculation					End of Year	
Year	Amortizable Cost	X	Amortization Rate	=	Amortization Expense	Accumulated Amortization	Net Book Value
2003							
2004							
2005							
2006							
2007							
2008							

(b) 2. Double Declining-Balance

	Calculation					End of Year	
Year	Net Book Value Begin. of Year	X	Amortization Rate	=	Amortization Expense	Accumulated Amortization	Net Book Value
2003							
2004							
2005							
2006							
2007							
2008							

(b) 3. Units-of-Activity

	Calculation					End of Year	
Year	Units of Activity	X	Amortization Cost/Unit	=	Amortization Expense	Accumulated Amortization	Net Book Value
2003							
2004							
2005							
2006							
2007							
2008							

(c) to (e)

(a)

(b) Straight-line

| | Calculation | | | | End of Year | |
Year	Amortizable Cost	X	Amortization Rate	=	Amortization Expense	Accumulated Amortization	Net Book Value
2004							
2005							
2006							
2007							
2008							

Name

Section

Date

Problem 9-5B

No.	Account Debited	Explanation

(a)

General Journal

Date	Account Titles and Explanation	Ref.	Debit	Credit

(b) and (c)

(a) 1. Straight-line

	Calculation				End of Year	
Year	Amortizable Cost	X	Amortization Rate	=	Amortization Expense	Accumulated Amortization	Net Book Value
1							
2							
3							

(a) 2. Units-of-Activity

	Calculation				End of Year	
Year	Units of Activity	X	Amortization Cost/Unit	=	Amortization Expense	Accumulated Amortization	Net Book Value
1							
2							
3							

(b)

	General Journal			
Date	Account Titles and Explanation	Ref.	Debit	Credit

(a)

General Journal

Date	Account Titles and Explanation	Ref.	Debit	Credit

(b)

(c)

	General Journal			
Date	Account Titles and Explanation	Ref.	Debit	Credit

(a) and (b)

General Journal

Date	Account Titles and Explanation	Ref.	Debit	Credit

P9-11B (c)

P9-12B (a)

General Journal

Date	Account Titles and Explanation	Ref.	Debit	Credit

(a) (Continued)

General Journal

Date	Account Titles and Explanation	Ref.	Debit	Credit

(b)

(a)

	St. Amand Company	St. Helene Company
Asset turnover		
Return on assets		

(b)

Part 1 (a)

General Journal

Date	Account Titles and Explanation	Ref.	Debit	Credit

(b) to (d)

Part 1 (e)

Part 2 (a)

(b) Straight-line

Year	Calculation				End of Year	
	Amortizable Cost	X	Amortization Rate	=	Amortization Expense	Accumulated Amortization	Net Book Value
2005						
2006						
2007						
2008						
2009						
2010						

(b) (Continued)

Double Declining-Balance

| Year | Calculation | | | | | End of Year | |
	Net Book Value Begin. of Year	X	Amortization Rate	=	Amortization Expense	Accumulated Amortization	Net Book Value
2005							
2006							
2007							
2008							
2009							
2010							

Units-of-Activity

| Year | Calculation | | | | | End of Year | |
	Units of Activity	X	Amortization Cost/Unit	=	Amortization Expense	Accumulated Amortization	Net Book Value
2005							
2006							
2007							
2008							
2009							
2010							

(c)

(d) to (f)

BE10-1			
1.		6.	
2.		7.	
3.		8.	
4.		9.	
5.		10.	

BE10-2 to 10-4

General Journal

Date	Account Titles and Explanation	Ref.	Debit	Credit

General Journal				
Date	Account Titles and Explanation	Ref.	Debit	Credit

BE10-8 to 10-10

General Journal

Date	Account Titles and Explanation	Ref.	Debit	Credit

BE10-10 (Arguments)

BE10-11

*BE10-12

*BE10-13 to 10-15

General Journal

Date	Account Titles and Explanation	Ref.	Debit	Credit

General Journal				
Date	Account Titles and Explanation	Ref.	Debit	Credit

General Journal				
Date	Account Titles and Explanation	Ref.	Debit	Credit

(a)

				General Journal

Date	Account Titles and Explanation	Ref.	Debit	Credit

(b)

	2005	2004

(c)

E10-6 and E10-7 (b) and (c)

General Journal

Date	Account Titles and Explanation	Ref.	Debit	Credit

E10-7 (a)

E10-8

E10-9

E10-10

	Assets	Liabilites	Owners' Equity	Revenues	Expenses	Net Income
1.	+	+	NE	NE	NE	NE
2.						
3.						
4.						
5.						
6.						
7.						
8.						
9.						
10.						
11.						

E10-11 (a)

E10-11 (b)

*E10-12

General Journal

Date	Account Titles and Explanation	Ref.	Debit	Credit

(a)

AHMAD COMPANY
Payroll Register
Week Ending January 31

| Employee | Total Hours | Gross Earnings | | | Deductions | | | | | Net Pay |
		Regular	Overtime	Gross Pay	CPP	EI	Income Tax	Health Insurance	Total	
A. Kassam										
H. Faas										
D. Liteplo										
Totals										

(b)

General Journal

Date	Account Titles and Explanation	Ref.	Debit	Credit

(a) and (b)

(c) and (d)

General Journal

Date	Account Titles and Explanation	Ref.	Debit	Credit

(a)

Transaction	Section	Account Title(s)	Amount(s)
1.			
2.			
3.			
..			
4.			
5.			
6.			
7.			

(b)

(a)

General Journal

Date	Account Titles and Explanation	Ref.	Debit	Credit

(b)

Notes Payable

Date	Explanation	Ref.	Debit	Credit	Balance
Jan. 1	Balance				12,000

Interest Payable

Date	Explanation	Ref.	Debit	Credit	Balance
Jan. 1	Balance				465

Interest Expense

Date	Explanation	Ref.	Debit	Credit	Balance

(c)

(a) and (b)

General Journal

Date	Account Titles and Explanation	Ref.	Debit	Credit

(a) and (b) (Continued)

General Journal

Date	Account Titles and Explanation	Ref.	Debit	Credit

(c)

General Journal				
Date	Account Titles and Explanation	Ref.	Debit	Credit

(a)

SURE VALUE HARDWARE
Payroll Register
Week Ending March 15, 2005

| Employee | Total Hours | Gross Earnings | | | Deductions | | | | | Net Pay | Store Wages Expense | Office Wages Expense |
		Regular	Overtime	Gross Pay	CPP	EI	Income Tax	United Way	Total			
I. Dahl												
F. Gualtieri												
G. Ho												
A. Israeli												
Totals												

(b) to (d)

General Journal

Date	Account Titles and Explanation	Ref.	Debit	Credit

(b)

General Journal

Date	Account Titles and Explanation	Ref.	Debit	Credit

(a) and (b)

Canada Pension Plan Payable

Date	Explanation	Ref.	Debit	Credit	Balance
Jan. 1	Balance				5,454

Employment Insurance Payable

Date	Explanation	Ref.	Debit	Credit	Balance
Jan. 1	Balance				2,923

Income Tax Payable

Date	Explanation	Ref.	Debit	Credit	Balance
Jan. 1	Balance				18,600

Workers' Compensation Payable

Date	Explanation	Ref.	Debit	Credit	Balance
Jan. 1	Balance				5,263

Union Dues Payable

Date	Explanation	Ref.	Debit	Credit	Balance
Jan. 1	Balance				1,250

Section _____

Date _____

(a) and (b) (Continued)

Canada Savings Bonds Payable

Date	Explanation	Ref.	Debit	Credit	Balance
Jan. 1	Balance				2,500

Vacation Pay Payable

Date	Explanation	Ref.	Debit	Credit	Balance
Jan. 1	Balance				6,450

Disability Insurance Payable

Date	Explanation	Ref.	Debit	Credit	Balance
Jan. 1	Balance				1,050

Salaries and Wages Payable

Date	Explanation	Ref.	Debit	Credit	Balance

(c)

(a) and (b)

General Journal

Date	Account Titles and Explanation	Ref.	Debit	Credit

(c)

Name

Section

Date

(a)

Transaction	Section	Account Title(s)	Amount(s)
1.			
2.			
3.			
4.			
5.			
6.			
7.			

(b)

(a)

General Journal

Date	Account Titles and Explanation	Ref.	Debit	Credit

(b)   Notes Payable

Date	Explanation	Ref.	Debit	Credit	Balance
Jan. 1	Balance				15,000

Interest Payable

Date	Explanation	Ref.	Debit	Credit	Balance
Jan. 1	Balance				375

Interest Expense

Date	Explanation	Ref.	Debit	Credit	Balance

(c)

(a) and (b)

General Journal

Date	Account Titles and Explanation	Ref.	Debit	Credit

(a) and (b) (Continued)

General Journal

Date	Account Titles and Explanation	Ref.	Debit	Credit

(c)

General Journal				
Date	Account Titles and Explanation	Ref.	Debit	Credit

(a)

SCOOT SCOOTERS
Payroll Register
Week Ending February 15, 2005

Employee	Total Hours	Gross Earnings			Deductions					Net Pay
		Regular	Overtime	Gross Pay	CPP	EI	Income Tax	United Way	Total	
P. Kilchyk										
B. Quon										
C. Pospisil										
B. Verwey										
Totals										

(b) to (d)

General Journal

Date	Account Titles and Explanation	Ref.	Debit	Credit

(b)

General Journal

Date	Account Titles and Explanation	Ref.	Debit	Credit

(a) and (b)

Canada Pension Plan Payable

Date	Explanation	Ref.	Debit	Credit	Balance
Jan. 1	Balance				8,788

Employment Insurance Payable

Date	Explanation	Ref.	Debit	Credit	Balance
Jan. 1	Balance				4,768

Income Tax Payable

Date	Explanation	Ref.	Debit	Credit	Balance
Jan. 1	Balance				25,510

Workers' Compensation Payable

Date	Explanation	Ref.	Debit	Credit	Balance
Jan. 1	Balance				5,676

Union Dues Payable

Date	Explanation	Ref.	Debit	Credit	Balance
Jan. 1	Balance				1,200

Section

Date

(a) and (b) (Continued)

Canada Savings Bonds Payable

Date	Explanation	Ref.	Debit	Credit	Balance
Jan. 1	Balance				2,420

Vacation Pay Payable

Date	Explanation	Ref.	Debit	Credit	Balance
Jan. 1	Balance				10,704

United Way Payable

Date	Explanation	Ref.	Debit	Credit	Balance
Jan. 1	Balance				750

Salaries and Wages Payable

Date	Explanation	Ref.	Debit	Credit	Balance
Jan. 1	Balance				0

(a)

(b) and (c)

General Journal

Date	Account Titles and Explanation	Ref.	Debit	Credit

Part 1

(a) and (d)

Warranty Liability

Date	Explanation	Ref	Debit	Credit	Balance

(b), (c), and (e)

General Journal

Date	Account Titles and Explanation	Ref.	Debit	Credit

_____

Part 2

(a)

(b) to (c)

General Journal

Date	Account Titles and Explanation	Ref.	Debit	Credit

(a)

General Journal

Date	Account Titles and Explanation	Ref.	Debit	Credit

(b)

(c)

(c) (Continued)

General Journal				
Date	Account Titles and Explanation	Ref.	Debit	Credit

General Journal				
Date	Account Titles and Explanation	Ref.	Debit	Credit

(a)

General Journal

Date	Account Titles and Explanation	Ref.	Debit	Credit

(b)

General Journal

Date	Account Titles and Explanation	Ref.	Debit	Credit

(c)

General Journal

Date	Account Titles and Explanation	Ref.	Debit	Credit

Name

Section

Date

(d)

General Journal

Date	Account Titles and Explanation	Ref.	Debit	Credit

(a)

General Journal

Date	Account Titles and Explanation	Ref.	Debit	Credit

(b)

General Journal

Date	Account Titles and Explanation	Ref.	Debit	Credit

Name _____

Section _____

Date _____

(c)

General Journal

Date	Account Titles and Explanation	Ref.	Debit	Credit

(d)

General Journal

Date	Account Titles and Explanation	Ref.	Debit	Credit

General Journal				
Date	Account Titles and Explanation	Ref.	Debit	Credit

General Journal				
Date	Account Titles and Explanation	Ref.	Debit	Credit

	General Journal			
Date	Account Titles and Explanation	Ref.	Debit	Credit

	General Journal			
Date	Account Titles and Explanation	Ref.	Debit	Credit

PB-2 Concluded

General Journal

Date	Account Titles and Explanation	Ref.	Debit	Credit

PB-3

General Journal

Date	Account Titles and Explanation	Ref.	Debit	Credit

General Journal				
Date	Account Titles and Explanation	Ref.	Debit	Credit

Section

Date

BEC-1 (a) Accounts Receivable Subsidiary Ledger

Duffy Co.

Date	Explanation	Ref.	Debit	Credit	Balance

Hanson Inc.

Date	Explanation	Ref.	Debit	Credit	Balance

Lewis Co.

Date	Explanation	Ref.	Debit	Credit	Balance

BEC-1 (b) General Ledger

Accounts Receivable

Date	Explanation	Ref.	Debit	Credit	Balance

BEC-2	
1.	4.
2.	5.
3.	6.

BEC-3	
1.	5.
2.	6.
3.	7.
4.	8.

BEC-4	(a) Journal	(b) Journal Columns
1.		
2.		
3.		
4.		
5.		
6.		
7.		
8.		
9.		

BEC-5	Journal	Column Titles
1.		
2.		
3.		
4.		
5.		
6.		
7.		
8.		

EC-1	
1.	7.
2.	8.
3.	9.
4.	10.
5.	11.
6.	12.

EC-2 (a) and (b)

SING TAO COMPANY

Sales Journal S1

Date	Account Debited	Invoice No.	Ref.	Accounts Receivable Dr. Sales Cr.	Cost of Goods Sold Dr. Merch. Inventory Cr.

EC-2 (a) and (c)

SING TAO COMPANY

Purchases Journal P1

Date	Account Credited	Terms	Ref.	Merchandise Inventory Dr. Accounts Payable Cr.

EC-3 (a) and (b)

SING TAO COMPANY

Cash Receipts Journal CR1

Date	Account Credited	Ref.	Cash Dr.	Accounts Receivable Cr.	Sales Cr.	CGS Dr. Merch. Inventory Cr.	Other Accounts Cr.

(a) and (c)

SING TAO COMPANY

Cash Payments Journal   CP1

Date	Ch. No.	Payee	Cash Cr.	Merch. Inventory Dr.	Accounts Payable Dr.	Account Debited	Ref.	Other Accounts Dr.

(a) and (d)   J1

General Journal

Date	Account Titles and Explanation	Ref.	Debit	Credit

(a)

General Journal

Date	Account Titles and Explanation	Ref.	Debit	Credit

(b)

To:

From:

Subject:

EC-5

EC-6 (a) and (b)

General Ledger

Accounts Receivable

Date	Explanation	Ref.	Debit	Credit	Balance
Sept. 1	Balance				11,960

Accounts Receivable Subsidiary Ledger

Bickford

Date	Explanation	Ref.	Debit	Credit	Balance
Sept. 1	Balance				4,820

(a) and (b) (Continued)

Cavanaugh

Date	Explanation	Ref.	Debit	Credit	Balance
Sept. 1	Balance				2,060

Iman

Date	Explanation	Ref.	Debit	Credit	Balance

Jana

Date	Explanation	Ref.	Debit	Credit	Balance
Sept. 1	Balance				2,440

Kingston

Date	Explanation	Ref.	Debit	Credit	Balance
Sept. 1	Balance				2,640

(c)

PIRIE COMPANY
Schedule of Customers
September 30, 2005

EC-7 (a) and (b)

SING TAO COMPANY

Sales Journal

S1

Date	Account Debited	Invoice No.	Ref.	Accounts Receivable Dr. Sales Cr.

EC-7 (a) and (c)

SING TAO COMPANY

Purchases Journal

P1

Date	Account Credited	Terms	Ref.	Purchases Dr. Accounts Payable Cr.

EC-8 (a) and (b)

SING TAO COMPANY

Cash Receipts Journal

CR1

Date	Account Credited	Ref.	Cash Dr.	Accounts Receivable Cr.	Sales Cr.	Other Accounts Cr.

EC-8 (a) and (c)

SING TAO COMPANY

Cash Payments Journal

CP1

Date	Ch. No.	Payee	Cash Cr.	Accounts Payable Dr.	Account Debited	Ref.	Other Accounts Dr.

(a) and (d)

General Journal   J1

Date	Account Titles and Explanation	Ref.	Debit	Credit

(a), (b) and (c)

Sales Journal S1

Date	Account Debited	Invoice No.	Ref.	Accounts Receivable Dr. Sales Cr.	Cost of Goods Sold Dr. Merch. Inventory Cr.

Purchases Journal P1

Date	Account Credited	Terms	Ref.	Merchandise Inventory Dr. Accounts Payable Cr.

General Journal J1

Date	Account Titles and Explanation	Ref.	Debit	Credit

(a), (b) and (c) (Continued)

Cash Receipts Journal   CR1

Date	Account Credited	Ref.	Cash Dr.	Accounts Receivable Cr.	Sales Cr.	CGS Dr. Merch. Inv. Cr.	Other Accounts Cr.

Cash Payments Journal   CP1

Date	Ch. No.	Payee	Cash Cr.	Merch. Inventory Dr.	Accounts Payable Dr.	Account Debited	Ref.	Other Accounts Dr.

(a), (b) and (c)

Sales Journal
S1

Date	Account Debited	Invoice No.	Ref.	Accounts Receivable Dr. Sales Cr.	Cost of Goods Sold Dr. Merch. Inventory Cr.

Purchases Journal
P1

Date	Account Credited	Terms	Ref.	Merchandise Inventory Dr. Accounts Payable Cr.

Cash Receipts Journal
CR1

Date	Account Credited	Ref.	Cash Dr.	Accounts Receivable Cr.	Sales Cr.	CGS Dr. Merch. Inventory Cr.	Other Accounts Cr.

(a), (b) and (c) (Continued)

Cash Payments Journal   CP1

Date	Ch. No.	Payee	Cash Cr.	Merch. Inventory Dr.	Accounts Paybale Dr.	Account Debited	Ref.	Other Accounts Dr.

General Journal   J1

Date	Account Titles and Explanation	Ref.	Debit	Credit

(b)   Sales Journal   S1

Date	Account Debited	Invoice No.	Ref.	Accounts Receivable Dr. Sales Cr.	Cost of Goods Sold Dr. Merch. Inventory Cr.

Purchases Journal   P1

Date	Account Credited	Terms	Ref.	Merchandise Inventory Dr. Accounts Payable Cr.

Cash Receipts Journal   CR1

Date	Account Credited	Ref.	Cash Dr.	Accounts Receivable Cr.	Sales Cr.	CGS Dr. Merch. Inventory Cr.	Other Accounts Cr.

(b) (Continued)

Cash Payments Journal   CP1

Date	Ch. No.	Payee	Cash Cr.	Merch. Inventory Dr.	Accounts Payable Dr.	Account Debited	Ref.	Other Accounts Dr.

General Journal   J1

Date	Account Titles and Explanation	Ref.	Debit	Credit

(a) and (c)

General Ledger

Cash   No. 101

Date	Explanation	Ref.	Debit	Credit	Balance
Jan. 1	Balance				49,500

Accounts Receivable   No. 112

Date	Explanation	Ref.	Debit	Credit	Balance
Jan. 1	Balance				15,000

Notes Receivable   No. 115

Date	Explanation	Ref.	Debit	Credit	Balance
Jan. 1	Balance				45,000

Merchandise Inventory   No. 120

Date	Explanation	Ref.	Debit	Credit	Balance
Jan. 1	Balance				22,000

Land   No. 140

Date	Explanation	Ref.	Debit	Credit	Balance
Jan. 1	Balance				25,000

(a) and (c) (Continued)

Building — No. 145

Date	Explanation	Ref.	Debit	Credit	Balance
Jan. 1	Balance				75,000

Accumulated Amortization - Building — No. 146

Date	Explanation	Ref.	Debit	Credit	Balance
Jan. 1	Balance				18,000

Equipment — No. 157

Date	Explanation	Ref.	Debit	Credit	Balance
Jan. 1	Balance				6,450

Accumulated Amortization - Equipment — No. 158

Date	Explanation	Ref.	Debit	Credit	Balance
Jan. 1	Balance				1,500

Notes Payable — No. 200

Date	Explanation	Ref.	Debit	Credit	Balance

Accounts Payable — No. 201

Date	Explanation	Ref.	Debit	Credit	Balance
Jan. 1	Balance				42,000

(a) and (c) (Continued)

Mortgage Payable   No. 275

Date	Explanation	Ref.	Debit	Credit	Balance
Jan. 1	Balance				82,000

M. Gibbs, Capital   No. 301

Date	Explanation	Ref.	Debit	Credit	Balance
Jan. 1	Balance				94,450

M. Gibbs, Drawings   No. 310

Date	Explanation	Ref.	Debit	Credit	Balance

Sales   No. 401

Date	Explanation	Ref.	Debit	Credit	Balance

Sales Returns and Allowances   No. 410

Date	Explanation	Ref.	Debit	Credit	Balance

Cost of Goods Sold   No. 505

Date	Explanation	Ref.	Debit	Credit	Balance

Salaries Expense   No. 725

Date	Explanation	Ref.	Debit	Credit	Balance

(a) and (c) (Continued)

Interest Revenue   No. 810

Date	Explanation	Ref.	Debit	Credit	Balance

Loss - Damaged Inventory   No. 920

Date	Explanation	Ref.	Debit	Credit	Balance

Accounts Receivable Subsidiary Ledger

S. Armstrong

Date	Explanation	Ref.	Debit	Credit	Balance
Jan. 1	Balance				4,500

R. Christof

Date	Explanation	Ref.	Debit	Credit	Balance
Jan. 1	Balance				3,000

B. Hibberd

Date	Explanation	Ref.	Debit	Credit	Balance
Jan. 1	Balance				7,500

B. Rhol

Date	Explanation	Ref.	Debit	Credit	Balance

(a) and (c) (Continued)

Accounts Payable Subsidiary Ledger

Fieldstone Corp.

Date	Explanation	Ref.	Debit	Credit	Balance
Jan. 1	Balance				9,000

Harms Distributors

Date	Explanation	Ref.	Debit	Credit	Balance
Jan. 1	Balance				16,000

Lapeska Co.

Date	Explanation	Ref.	Debit	Credit	Balance
Jan. 1	Balance				1,900

Warren Parts Co.

Date	Explanation	Ref.	Debit	Credit	Balance

Watson & Co.

Date	Explanation	Ref.	Debit	Credit	Balance
Jan. 1					17,000

(d)

	Debit	Credit

Name

Section

Date

(e)

(b)   Sales Journal   S1

Date	Account Debited	Invoice No.	Ref.	Accounts Receivable Dr. Sales Cr.	CGS Dr. Merch. Inventory Cr.

Purchases Journal   P1

Date	Account Credited	Terms	Ref.	Merchandise Inventory Dr. Accounts Payable Cr.

General Journal   J1

Date	Account Titles and Explanation	Ref.	Debit	Credit

Cash Receipts Journal   CR1

Date	Account Credited	Ref.	Cash Dr.	Accounts Receivable Cr.	Sales Cr.	CGS Dr. Merch. Inventory Cr.	Other Accounts Cr.

(b) (Continued)

Cash Payments Journal

CP1

Date	Ch. No.	Payee	Cash Cr.	Merch. Inventory Dr.	Accounts Payable Dr.	Account Debited	Ref.	Other Accounts Dr.

(a) and (c)

General Ledger

Cash

No. 101

Date	Explanation	Ref.	Debit	Credit	Balance
May 1	Balance				36,700

Accounts Receivable

No. 112

Date	Explanation	Ref.	Debit	Credit	Balance
May 1	Balance				15,400

Notes Receivable

No. 115

Date	Explanation	Ref.	Debit	Credit	Balance
May 1	Balance				48,000

(a) and (c) (Continued)

Merchandise Inventory   No. 120

Date	Explanation	Ref.	Debit	Credit	Balance
May 1	Balance				22,000

Equipment   No. 157

Date	Explanation	Ref.	Debit	Credit	Balance
May 1	Balance				8,200

Accumulated Amortization - Equipment   No. 158

Date	Explanation	Ref.	Debit	Credit	Balance
May 1	Balance				1,800

Notes Payable   No. 200

Date	Explanation	Ref.	Debit	Credit	Balance

Accounts Payable   No. 201

Date	Explanation	Ref.	Debit	Credit	Balance
May 1	Balance				43,400

C. Scholz, Capital   No. 301

Date	Explanation	Ref.	Debit	Credit	Balance
May 1	Balance				85,100

(a) and (c) (Continued)

C. Scholz, Drawings   No. 310

Date	Explanation	Ref.	Debit	Credit	Balance

Sales   No. 401

Date	Explanation	Ref.	Debit	Credit	Balance

Sales Returns and Allowances   No. 410

Date	Explanation	Ref.	Debit	Credit	Balance

Cost of Goods Sold   No. 505

Date	Explanation	Ref.	Debit	Credit	Balance

Salaries Expense   No. 725

Date	Explanation	Ref.	Debit	Credit	Balance

Rent Expense   No. 730

Date	Explanation	Ref.	Debit	Credit	Balance

Interest Revenue   No. 810

Date	Explanation	Ref.	Debit	Credit	Balance

(a) and (c) (Continued)

Accounts Receivable Subsidiary Ledger

L. Cellars

Date	Explanation	Ref.	Debit	Credit	Balance
May 1	Balance				7,400

W. Karasch

Date	Explanation	Ref.	Debit	Credit	Balance
May 1	Balance				3,250

G. Parrish

Date	Explanation	Ref.	Debit	Credit	Balance
May 1	Balance				4,750

B. Simone

Date	Explanation	Ref.	Debit	Credit	Balance

Accounts Payable Subsidiary Ledger

Buttercup Distributors

Date	Explanation	Ref.	Debit	Credit	Balance
May 1	Balance				17,400

Elite Sports

Date	Explanation	Ref.	Debit	Credit	Balance
May 1	Balance				15,500

Name _____   Problem C-4 Continued
Section _____
Date _____

(a) and (c) (Continued)

Lancio Co.

Date	Explanation	Ref.	Debit	Credit	Balance

Werner Widgits

Date	Explanation	Ref.	Debit	Credit	Balance

Winterware Corp.

Date	Explanation	Ref.	Debit	Credit	Balance
May 1	Balance				10,500

(d)

	Debit	Credit

(e)

(a), (b) and (c)   Sales Journal   S1

Date	Account Debited	Invoice No.	Ref.	Accounts Receivable Dr. Sales Cr.

Purchases Journal   P1

Date	Account Credited	Terms	Ref.	Purchases Dr. Accounts Payable Cr.

General Journal   J1

Date	Account Titles and Explanation	Ref.	Debit	Credit

(a), (b) and (c) (Continued)

Cash Receipts Journal CR1

Date	Account Credited	Ref.	Cash Dr.	Accounts Receivable Cr.	Sales Cr.	Other Accounts Cr.

Cash Payments Journal CP1

Date	Ch. No.	Payee	Cash Cr.	Accounts Payable Dr.	Account Debited	Ref.	Other Accounts Dr.

(a)   Sales Journal   S1

Date	Account Debited	Invoice No.	Ref.	Accounts Receivable Dr. Sales Cr.	CGS Dr. Merch. Inventory Cr.

                               Purchases Journal   P1

Date	Account Credited	Terms	Ref.	Merchandise Inventory Dr. Accounts Payable Cr.

Name

Section

Date

(a) (Continued)

Cash Receipts Journal — CR1

Date	Account Credited	Ref.	Cash Dr.	Accounts Receivable Cr.	Sales Cr.	CGS Dr. Merch. Inv. Cr.	Other Accounts Dr.

Cash Payments Journal — CP1

Date	Ch. No.	Payee	Cash Cr.	Merch. Inventory Dr.	Accounts Payable Dr.	Account Debited	Ref.	Other Accounts Dr.

(a), (d) and (f)

General Journal   J1

Date	Account Titles and Explanation	Ref.	Debit	Credit

(a), (d) and (f) (Continued)

General Journal   J2

Date	Account Titles and Explanation	Ref.	Debit	Credit

(b) and (f)

Cash   No. 101

Date	Explanation	Ref.	Debit	Credit	Balance
Jan. 1	Balance				35,050

Accounts Receivable   No. 112

Date	Explanation	Ref.	Debit	Credit	Balance
Jan. 1	Balance				14,000

Notes Receivable   No. 115

Date	Explanation	Ref.	Debit	Credit	Balance
Jan. 1	Balance				39,000

Merchandise Inventory   No. 120

Date	Explanation	Ref.	Debit	Credit	Balance
Jan. 1	Balance				20,000

Office Supplies   No. 125

Date	Explanation	Ref.	Debit	Credit	Balance
Jan. 1	Balance				1,000

(b) and (f) (Continued)

Prepaid Insurance   No. 130

Date	Explanation	Ref.	Debit	Credit	Balance
Jan. 1	Balance				2,000

Land   No. 140

Date	Explanation	Ref.	Debit	Credit	Balance
Jan. 1	Balance				50,000

Building   No. 145

Date	Explanation	Ref.	Debit	Credit	Balance
Jan. 1	Balance				100,000

Accumulated Amortization - Building   No. 146

Date	Explanation	Ref.	Debit	Credit	Balance
Jan. 1	Balance				25,000

Equipment   No. 157

Date	Explanation	Ref.	Debit	Credit	Balance
Jan. 1	Balance				6,450

Accumulated Amortization - Equipment   No. 158

Date	Explanation	Ref.	Debit	Credit	Balance
Jan. 1	Balance				1,500

Notes Payable   No. 200

Date	Explanation	Ref.	Debit	Credit	Balance

(b) and (f) (Continued)

Accounts Payable   No. 201

Date	Explanation	Ref.	Debit	Credit	Balance
Jan. 1	Balance				36,000

Interest Payable   No. 230

Date	Explanation	Ref.	Debit	Credit	Balance

Mortgage Payable   No. 275

Date	Explanation	Ref.	Debit	Credit	Balance
Jan. 1	Balance				125,000

Income Summary   No. 300

Date	Explanation	Ref.	Debit	Credit	Balance

A. Kassam, Capital   No. 301

Date	Explanation	Ref.	Debit	Credit	Balance
Jan. 1	Balance				80,000

A. Kassam, Drawings   No. 306

Date	Explanation	Ref.	Debit	Credit	Balance

(b) and (f) (Continued)

Sales   No. 401

Date	Explanation	Ref.	Debit	Credit	Balance

Sales Returns and Allowances   No. 410

Date	Explanation	Ref.	Debit	Credit	Balance

Cost of Goods Sold   No. 505

Date	Explanation	Ref.	Debit	Credit	Balance

Loss - Inventory Shrinkage   No. 506

Date	Explanation	Ref.	Debit	Credit	Balance

Amortization Expense   No. 711

Date	Explanation	Ref.	Debit	Credit	Balance

Interest Expense   No. 718

Date	Explanation	Ref.	Debit	Credit	Balance

(b) and (f) (Continued)

Insurance Expense   No. 722

Date	Explanation	Ref.	Debit	Credit	Balance

Salaries Expense   No. 725

Date	Explanation	Ref.	Debit	Credit	Balance

Office Supplies Expense   No. 728

Date	Explanation	Ref.	Debit	Credit	Balance

(b) and (f) (Continued)

Accounts Receivable Subsidiary Ledger

R. Draves

Date	Explanation	Ref.	Debit	Credit	Balance
Jan. 1	Balance				1,500

J. Ebel

Date	Explanation	Ref.	Debit	Credit	Balance

B. Jacovetti

Date	Explanation	Ref.	Debit	Credit	Balance
Jan. 1	Balance				7,500

S. Kysely

Date	Explanation	Ref.	Debit	Credit	Balance
Jan. 1	Balance				5,000

(b) and (f) (Continued)

Accounts Payable Subsidiary Ledger

Laux Supplies

Date	Explanation	Ref.	Debit	Credit	Balance

Liazuk Co.

Date	Explanation	Ref.	Debit	Credit	Balance
Jan. 1	Balance				10,000

Mikush Bros.

Date	Explanation	Ref.	Debit	Credit	Balance
Jan. 1	Balance				15,000

Nguyen & Son

Date	Explanation	Ref.	Debit	Credit	Balance
Jan. 1	Balance				11,000

Welz Wares

Date	Explanation	Ref.	Debit	Credit	Balance

(c) and (d)

	Unadjusted		Adjusted	
	Debit	Credit	Debit	Credit

(c) (Continued)

(e)

(e) (Continued)

(g)

	Debit	Credit

NOTES

NOTES

NOTES

NOTES

NOTES

NOTES

NOTES

NOTES

NOTES

NOTES

NOTES